RETAINING NEW TEACHERS

*How do I support and develop
novice teachers?*

BRYAN
HARRIS

ASCD   Alexandria, VA USA

Website: www.ascd.org
E-mail: books@ascd.org

www.ascdarias.org

Printed in the United States of America. Cover art © 2015 by ASCD. ASCD publications present a variety of viewpoints. The views expressed or implied in this book should not be interpreted as official positions of the Association.

PAPERBACK ISBN: 978-1-4166-2058-7   ASCD product #SF115054
Also available as an e-book (see Books in Print for the ISBNs).

Library of Congress Cataloging-in-Publication Data
Harris, Bryan (Teacher)
  Retaining new teachers : how do I support and develop novice teachers? / Bryan Harris.
      pages cm
  Includes bibliographical references and index.
  ISBN 978-1-4166-2058-7 (pbk. : alk. paper) 1. First year teachers—United States. 2. Mentoring in education—United States. 3. Teachers—Selection and appointment—United States. 4. Teacher turnover—United States. I. Title.
  LB2844.1.N4H37 2015
  371.1020973—dc23
                              2015002498

21 20 19 18 17 16 15   1 2 3 4 5 6 7 8 9 10 11 12

RETAINING NEW TEACHERS

How do I support and develop novice teachers?

Want to earn a free ASCD Arias e-book?
Your opinion counts! Please take 2–3 minutes to give
us your feedback on this publication. All survey
respondents will be entered into a drawing to
win an ASCD Arias e-book.

Please visit
www.ascd.org/ariasfeedback

Thank you!

Introduction

It's a national disgrace: up to half of all new teachers leave the profession within their first three to five years (Ingersoll & Strong, 2011). Across the country, thousands of teaching positions are going unfilled or are being filled by less-than-qualified teachers. Why does this teacher shortage persist, and what can we do about it? How would we react, as a nation, if up to half of all *students* dropped out of school at the same rate?

Education leaders must wake up and take action—before we fail an entire generation of teachers and their students. That's where this book comes in. In these pages, I provide specific, practical action points for creating supports and programs that will encourage new teachers to remain in the profession and ensure that they experience success early on. This book is intended for school and district leaders, policy-makers, veteran teachers, and anyone else who has an interest in fostering early-career teachers' success and retention.

The Problem of High Attrition for Early-Career Teachers

Despite much research (see, for example, Ingersoll & Strong, 2011) on the factors that influence new-teacher retention, attrition rates continue to be frighteningly high. Looking at the annual attrition rates for new teachers in the last two decades, it is hard not to conclude that we have reached the state of a national crisis. There is growing concern among teacher leaders, administrators, and policymakers that, unless we give specific attention to this problem, new teachers will continue to leave at high rates. A profession that does not support its newest recruits cannot stay a viable profession for long.

U.S. public schools are at a critical crossroads. It is estimated that an additional 200,000 teachers will be needed in the next decade because of such factors as the large wave of teacher retirement, an increase in immigration of school-age children, and the rising popularity of class-size reduction initiatives (Graue & Rauscher, 2009; Zumwalt & Craig, 2005). Compounding the problem is the failure of some states and regions to produce enough college graduates to meet the demand for new teachers. Many school districts attempt to fill these gaps by recruiting new teachers from other states. Unfortunately, these teachers tend to leave the profession at even higher rates than do those who don't make interstate moves to launch their careers (Harris, 2013). Even more alarming is the fact that some districts are compelled to hire teachers from other *countries*. What does it say about the United States that we can't produce enough qualified teachers to educate our children?

Why New Teachers Leave

Any discussion of new-teacher attrition must begin with the question *Why do these teachers leave in the first place?* Only after considering the answers to this question will we be able to create programs and supports that will get teachers to stay.

The following list, drawing from the findings of such well-known researchers as Linda Darling-Hammond (2005), Richard Ingersoll (2001), and Michael Strong (2005), highlights some of the major reasons new teachers leave their positions.

- **Relocation or migration.** Plenty of early-career teachers simply move to other schools or districts. Although these teachers stay in the profession, the communities they leave experience teacher attrition. The national trend is that teachers migrate away from higher-poverty communities toward wealthier ones (Ingersoll, 2001).
- **Career change.** Not everyone enters teaching with the plan to make it a lifelong career. Teaching may

end up being only one of several careers a person may have, especially among the Millennial generation. In addition, with the exception of administration, the education profession offers few opportunities for advancement for those who like to change jobs often or take on new challenges (Strong, 2005).

- **Job change or relocation of a spouse, family member, or significant other.** There are times when a teacher wants to stay in his or her current location but must move owing to family obligations.
- **Lifestyle change.** Some teachers leave the profession to make a lifestyle change, such as becoming a full-time parent or taking care of a sick family member.
- **Being counseled out of the profession.** All healthy organizations weed out the poorest-performing employees. Sometimes, despite a school's best efforts to provide support, an individual just does not develop the skills to be an effective teacher. In such cases, it is beneficial to students and to the school for them to move on to different careers.
- **Poor pay and benefits.** Without going into a tangent on school funding and teacher salaries, suffice it to say that it can be challenging to make ends meet on the typical new-teacher pay. Many early-career teachers recently graduated from college, where they were financially sheltered with loans or support from parents. It can be a rude awakening to suddenly bear the full load of their financial obligations, and the realization of just how little they bring home

each month drives some novice teachers to seek higher-paying careers. Although it is a political hot-button issue in many parts of the country, increasing beginning teachers' pay will go a long way toward retaining good teachers.

- **Inadequate resources.** To do their job effectively, teachers need more than just a sufficient paycheck. They need up-to-date technology, current textbooks, professional development, and access to service providers like school psychologists and counselors. National and state legislators as well as communities need to recognize that a lack of these resources, in addition to inadequate pay, leads some new teachers to pursue other careers.

- **High stress and lack of support.** It's a sad fact: not all schools are designed to support new teachers. Some veteran teachers and administrators have adopted the mindset that new teachers just have to figure it out on their own. After all, *they* had to tough it out and learn how to survive the system, so why shouldn't the new ones? Unfortunately, the stress of trying to become an effective teacher without receiving any support leads many teachers to seek a more supportive environment. In the best-case scenarios, they move on to more supportive schools. In the worst-case scenarios, they assume all schools have a sink-or-swim philosophy and leave the profession entirely.

- **Difficult working conditions.** Although it may seem counterintuitive, many new teachers receive more challenging teaching loads than do their experienced colleagues. Sometimes they are assigned a greater number of students who exhibit behavior problems or have special needs. Often, they are given a wider selection of topics to teach because the veteran teachers in the system have "earned" a more flexible and focused teaching schedule. In addition, many new teachers are tasked with coaching sports teams, advising clubs, and other after-school duties that add to their stress. These working conditions can quickly lead to burnout.

- **"Bashing" of the teaching profession.** The institution of public education has sadly become ground zero for many political debates that have little grounding in truth or evidence. Make no mistake: as a nation, we *should* engage in honest debate about how best to educate our children. There are many, however, who have taken this debate as an opportunity to blame educators for all the ills of society. The fact is that schools reflect the problems of society; they don't create them. The political environment of "teacher bashing," or blaming educators for all the problems in schools (while ignoring the influence of major factors like poverty), has a negative effect on the mindset of current and would-be teachers. Gerald Tirozzi, former executive director of the National Association of Secondary School Principals, understated the problem when he declared, "Decisions regarding becoming a teacher, or remaining in teaching as a profession, are diminished in such an environment" (Tirozzi, Carbonaro, & Winters, 2014).

These are the main reasons early-career teachers leave the profession. Although some factors are clearly out of our control, others stem from dysfunction within the profession that we can and should address. The natural follow-up question is, *What influences a new teacher's decision to stay in the profession?* To some extent, we can take the list above and just turn it around. For example, we can increase pay for new teachers and provide them with opportunities for advancement within the profession. However, even those factors are often beyond the control of school-based leaders.

Four Supports That Make a Difference

The good news is that there are still many things school leaders and policymakers can do to retain new teachers— and, just as important, to help them and their students succeed. There is a wealth of data and research (Ingersoll & Strong, 2011) pointing to programs and practices that can help retain and support early-career teachers. The following sections discuss four crucial factors: *comprehensive induction programs, supportive administrators, skilled mentors,* and *helpful colleagues*. When effectively combined, these broad areas of support greatly increase the likelihood that new teachers will remain—and thrive—in the profession.

Induction Programs

> **KEY IDEA:** New teachers who participate in a comprehensive induction program stay in the profession longer and experience greater success in terms of job satisfaction and student achievement (Bartlett & Johnson, 2010; Ingersoll & Strong, 2011).

To combat high attrition rates among novice teachers, school districts have been increasingly relying on induction programs to assist new teachers with their transition into the profession. A majority of new teachers in the United States now participate in some sort of induction program (Ingersoll & Strong, 2011). Many states and numerous independent organizations have developed and published standards to guide schools and districts in the induction process.

Broadly defined, *induction* refers to a range of support structures, programs, strategies, and trainings specifically designed to assist new teachers during their first few years in the profession. Although induction programs have many declared goals, they most often serve three basic purposes:

1. To provide instruction in classroom management and effective teaching techniques.

2. To ease the difficulty of the transition into teaching.

3. To maximize the retention rate of new teachers. (Breaux & Wong, 2003)

High-quality, comprehensive induction programs typically have several elements in common. The following list—based on the work of leading experts in the field, including Richard Ingersoll and Thomas Smith (Smith & Ingersoll, 2004), Michael Strong (2005), Ellen Moir (2009), and Linda Darling-Hammond (2005)—serves as an excellent starting point for designing or evaluating an induction program. Although not designed to be comprehensive, this list provides an overview of the essential features of an effective induction program. Successful programs

- **Have a multiyear focus.** New teachers need support during the first several years of their career. Although the greatest amount of support is typically offered during the first year (often via several days of induction and training prior to the beginning of the school year), new teachers benefit from support during at least their first three years.
- **Incorporate an induction "week."** Although the number of days varies, effective induction programs start with several days (typically two to five) of training specially designed for new teachers. Many districts begin this induction week with a special rally, kick-off event, or breakfast where new teachers are welcomed into the district and community.
- **Include an orientation to the school, district, and community.** Many new teachers are new to the state or district they will be working in, so induction activities should orient teachers to the school and community. This orientation should also include

detailed information about the school or district's mission and vision.

- **Assign mentors.** A core element found in the majority of induction programs is the assignment of a mentor for the new teacher (Fulton, Yoon, & Lee, 2005). Mentors are asked to serve a variety of roles, ranging from informal emotional support to formal classroom observations (Strong, 2005). We will examine mentoring in greater depth on pages 21–28.
- **Provide strong administrative support.** Every level of administrative leadership—from the superintendent to site principals—needs to understand the importance of supporting new teachers. Individuals in leadership positions, including governing board members, must support and, whenever possible, participate in some elements of the induction process.
- **Are led by individuals who are trained in the needs of new teachers.** The individuals and teams who lead the induction process should be knowledgeable and empathetic about the specific needs of new teachers and available to help them during their transition into the profession. Induction leaders should be chosen only after careful consideration because they will be the new teachers' very first models of professionalism, communication, and collegiality.
- **Address issues of particular need for new teachers.** Although topics such as health insurance, benefits, and how to access the district's e-mail system are

important, they are not the most important topics to address during induction. Effective induction programs recognize that new teachers are typically concerned about classroom management, student behavior, organization, lesson planning, and instruction. Accordingly, leaders should structure induction experiences so that they meet those needs. In particular, new teachers benefit from training in the specific instructional methodologies (including lesson planning) and classroom management techniques used within the school or district.

- **Prioritize professional growth and reflective practice.** Increasingly, schools and districts are expecting new teachers to take an active role in their own professional growth. Rather than merely providing a list of required trainings and meetings to attend, administrators should grant new teachers some control in directing their own development. This may mean that a new teacher decides which professional learning opportunities to participate in and when to participate in them. Providing this level of control and freedom is empowering and accords with the new teacher's desire to be viewed as a professional.

The following action points, developed for administrators and key policymakers, will benefit new teachers as they become familiar with their new community, school, and district.

☐ **Give neighborhood tours.** One practical way to address the needs of new teachers is to provide information about the culture, background, and unique characteristics of the community they'll be teaching in. One practice, highlighted in Breaux and Wong's (2003) *New Teacher Induction,* is to arrange neighborhood tours for new teachers. In such tours, school administrators drive new teachers through the neighborhoods that surround the school, providing the teachers with firsthand information about the school, its students, and any challenges they may face when serving students. Depending on the new teachers' backgrounds, it may also help them move beyond what Huisman, Singer, and Catapano (2010) describe as the "mono-culture" many teachers experienced in their own K–16 education.

☐ **Encourage administrators and mentors to participate in induction activities.** When new teachers see that their principals, district-level leaders, and mentors view induction activities as important and valuable, they will be more likely to fully invest in the learning. In addition, school leaders' presence at these activities helps provide a common language and experience that can be a point of reference and reflection throughout the school year.

☐ **Create model classrooms.** Many districts ask select veteran teachers to set up their classrooms as they would for the first day of school and invite new teachers to visit and see how experienced teachers deal with desk arrangement, bulletin boards and focus walls, technology, organization of supplies, first-day-of-school activities, and so on. New teachers benefit greatly from seeing concrete examples on which they can model their own classrooms. For example, instead of merely hearing a description of the instructional technology available to them, new teachers can see how a veteran teacher actually puts the technology to use.

☐ **Balance classroom time and trainings.** It's important to keep in mind that new teachers' primary goal is to get their classrooms ready for the first day of school. Although it may seem most time-effective to fill their entire induction schedule with meetings and trainings, the training could well fall on deaf ears (or distracted minds) if teachers don't have sufficient time to set up their classrooms. Remember that many of them have never prepared a classroom on their own before, so it may take them more time and effort than it would for veteran teachers. Make sure to provide time during induction for new teachers to work in their classrooms.

The majority of new teachers' questions and needs will focus on the practical, not the theoretical. At the beginning of the year, most new teachers will be more concerned about desk arrangement and bulletin-board design than about reviewing student achievement data from the previous year. This is normal and should not be taken to mean that new teachers do not care about data, curricular materials, technology integration, or assessment. It just means that most teachers need to dispatch the immediate, utilitarian tasks before they feel able to tackle the larger, less tangible issues.

☐ **Hold beginning-teacher meetings.** Throughout their first few years in the profession, new teachers benefit from periodic meetings and training sessions that focus specifically on issues they face day to day. Topics such as student behavior, classroom management, parental communication, organization, lesson planning, and stress management are of particular concern to early-career teachers.

☐ **Arrange for observations.** New teachers profit greatly from the opportunity to observe the craft of their mentors and other veteran colleagues. During their first several years in the profession, new teachers should have the opportunity to regularly observe other, more experienced teachers. Often, principals, site-based academic coaches, or mentors join the new teachers during these observations.

Here is the big picture: effective induction programs go beyond mere orientation on the procedures and mission of a school district. They do not focus solely on informing new teachers about health benefits and how to use the district's system for reporting absences. Rather, they create a range of experiences, supports, and resources that help new teachers experience success and gain confidence during their transition into the profession.

Supportive Administrators

KEY IDEA: The support that principals, assistant principals, and other administrators provide to new teachers is critical to teachers' decision to remain in the education profession—or to leave it. Specifically, site-level administrative support from the principal has been described as "pivotal" in terms of an early-career teacher's success (Markow & Martin, 2005; Reiman & Corbell, 2007).

Site-level and district-level administrators alike have few priorities that are more important than ensuring the success and effectiveness of new teachers. Considering the current nationwide teacher shortage, it is essential that administrators give early-career teachers the support they need to thrive in the profession. We cannot afford, financially or otherwise, to keep losing such a high percentage of our new teachers.

Before considering specific steps they can take to support new teachers, leaders should do some self-reflection to consider the skills and behaviors that novice teachers most value in their administrators. The following list, compiled from sources such as the Center for Teaching Quality, the New Teacher Project, and the Metlife Survey of the American Teacher (Markow & Martin, 2005), includes some of these key characteristics and practices. An effective, respected administrator

- Is well organized.
- Recognizes teachers' accomplishments.
- Provides opportunities for advancement and teacher leadership.
- Shows a willingness to listen and provide feedback.
- Is highly visible and accessible.
- Has a vision for the school and can clearly communicate it.
- Appreciates the talents and enthusiasm of new staff.
- Intentionally creates opportunities for new and veteran staff to work together.
- Provides necessary resources, supplies, tools, and curriculum.
- Frequently spends time in classrooms for both formal and informal observations.

New teachers crave support, "face time," and guidance from their leaders. However, many teachers report a significant gap between the level of support they believe is essential for their success and what they actually receive from administrators (Harris, 2013). The following list includes concrete, practical ways in which principals and other administrators can support new teachers.

☐ **Assess school culture.** Kardos, Johnson, Peske, Kauffman, and Liu (2001) conducted seminal research on the impact of school culture on a variety of factors, including the retention of new teachers. They found that most school cultures fall into one of three categories: *veteran-oriented, novice-oriented,* or *integrated.* As might be expected, neither veteran-oriented nor novice-oriented cultures meet the needs of new teachers. It is only in integrated school cultures that new teachers get the support they need from leadership and veteran colleagues. The researchers found that new teachers who experienced an integrated culture were more likely to stay in the profession than were those who taught in a veteran-oriented or novice-oriented culture. Integrated cultures are characterized by administrators' openness to learning from and with new teachers. In an integrated culture, new teachers are granted special status while simultaneously receiving recognition as professionals who can contribute to the school's goals and mission.

☐ **Don't try to do it alone.** Barth (2013) reminds administrators that the job of school leadership is too complex to be done alone and suggests that principals and teacher leaders share the load to meet the needs of all school staff members. More specifically, Darling-Hammond (2013) suggests that principals seek the assistance of veterans and teacher teams to observe and provide feedback to new teachers. This approach is consistent with what Kardos and colleagues (2001) describe as the strength of an integrated professional culture.

☐ **Maintain realistic expectations.** Understand and accept that it is the rare novice teacher who has the skills to match his or her enthusiasm. This is normal, and it is true for most educators: most of us were not effective from day one. New teachers typically struggle with some aspects of classroom management, student behavior, organization, or communication. They need help to learn how to balance all the demands of the profession. Although we certainly don't want to tolerate or ignore ineffective practices with the hope that "they'll figure it out eventually," we should remain realistic and understand that becoming an effective teacher takes time.

☐ **Create sound bites.** All teachers will benefit from leaders who are able to articulate succinctly their beliefs about effective, appropriate instruction and classroom management. For example, when it comes to an issue like student engagement, school leadership should be able to clearly define and provide examples of what it means to engage students. Keep these definitions and examples short, concrete, and specific.

☐ **Hold new-teacher meetings.** Starting at the very beginning of the school year, schedule regular informal meetings with new teachers. Use these meetings as an opportunity to listen, share insights, and get to know the new teachers on a personal level. Although the meetings should be treated as a priority, they do not need to be especially formal or include an official agenda. Rather, these meetings give new teachers and the principal a chance to get to know and understand each other better. Use the meetings as an opportunity to share your vision and goals, recognize successes, and give teachers information about upcoming events. When scheduling, be sensitive to the demands that teachers may be facing during any particular week to avoid overwhelming them with yet another meeting.

☐ **Increase "face time."** In addition to holding regular meetings with new teachers, ensure that they have regular, positive interactions—what could be referred to as "face time"—with school leadership. Although the support that mentors and colleagues provide is very influential, new teachers value few things as much as personal, one-on-one time with their principal, when they can informally interact and get feedback and insights on such topics as classroom management, parent communication, and lesson planning. Effective principals don't consider new-teacher support a burdensome aspect of their work; on the contrary, they appreciate the vitality and enthusiasm that new teachers often bring to their school and embrace the opportunity to work with them.

☐ **Conduct instructional rounds.** One way for principals to increase face time is to partner with new teachers in observing the classroom practice of more experienced teachers. One such method, popularized by the work done at Harvard's Graduate School of Education and based on the practice of medical doctors, is called *instructional rounds*. During these rounds, school leaders and veteran educators team up with their less experienced colleagues for classroom visits and observations. During this time, novice educators are provided with models, coaching, feedback, and a chance to debrief about what they observe in classrooms.

☐ **Clarify roles of other support providers.** In addition to providing a formal mentor, many schools and districts provide early-career teachers with a host of other support personnel, often including a site-based academic coach, a district-based specialist, assistant principals, counselors, and grade-level or content-area chairs. All of these individuals have an agenda of important items they want to discuss with new teachers. Keep in mind, however, that not all issues are equally important, and it is very easy to overwhelm new teachers. Meet with these personnel (without the new teachers present) to clarify what each of them will be asking the new teachers to do, and when. Encourage the team to take into consideration the time demands and expectations that will be placed on the new teachers and make adjustments accordingly. Help everyone remember that the goal is to support new teachers so that they and their students experience success, not simply to have the teachers complete a bunch of requirements or tasks. Although it may be difficult to have too much *support*, it's easy to have too many *people* trying to provide that support.

☐ **Refer to them as full-fledged professionals.** Understand that novice teachers want to be fully accepted and acknowledged as professionals. Most of them, of course, realize that they have much to learn, but they have a desire to be appreciated and recognized for their educational accomplishments. Accordingly, both in public and in private, refer to them as the professionals they are. Refrain from highlighting their relative inexperience by referring to them as "rookies" or by making comments like "You're just in your first year." Statements like these can inadvertently give the impression that they are not as valued or important as veteran staff.

☐ **Earmark additional resources.** Whenever possible, provide new teachers with additional resources in the form of release time for planning or professional development, additional funds to purchase classroom materials, classroom aides, and technical assistance for performing tasks such as testing and completing progress reports.

☐ **Reduce class sizes and duty schedules.** Research (Darling-Hammond & Sykes, 2003) suggests that job dissatisfaction resulting from a heavy workload is a factor in new-teacher attrition. New teachers are sometimes given the most difficult teaching assignments and workloads on campus. Is it any wonder that so many of them leave within their first few years? School administrators can support the development of early-career teachers by sheltering them from the full range of responsibilities expected of veteran staff. For example, it would benefit most new teachers to experience a reduced class size during their first year of teaching and to be given fewer extra-duty tasks like playground duty and after-school coaching.

This may be a cause of contention among veteran teachers, so explain the rationale for these adjustments and ask veteran staff members to consider that education is one of the few professions that expects novices to perform at the same level as experienced educators—and it makes very little sense. It takes time, feedback, and support to perform effectively. Some veteran teachers, without even realizing it, have adopted a hazing mindset when it comes to their newest colleagues (*If I had to suffer through my first few years, they should, too*). Encourage veterans to examine this mindset more closely by asking them, "If we don't do something differently to support our new teachers, won't we continue to experience high turnover?" or "When you were a new teacher, how would you have benefited from a reduced workload?"

Finally, consider how you will respond if a new teacher volunteers for extra duties such as after-school coaching or tutoring. This is a delicate balance because many of them need the extra money, but the additional stress may impact their effectiveness in the classroom. Consider whether they are doing well enough in their "day job" to take on the additional responsibilities.

☐ **Create opportunities for collaboration.** Collaboration between novice and veteran teachers has a positive influence on new-teacher retention (Kardos & Johnson, 2007). Because school leaders have the primary responsibility to create conditions that allow for effective collaboration, they should take specific steps to ensure that the collaboration time is well spent. Simply giving teachers time to meet doesn't guarantee that meaningful collaboration will take place. Rather, school leaders must be intentional about creating expectations and circumstances that result in collaborative work. This means that in addition to providing the *time* to collaborate, principals must also provide the framework for *how* to collaborate, including expected outcomes, the norms by which groups should work, and the resources necessary to be successful. Principals should also make it a priority to regularly attend these collaboration meetings to ensure that the new teachers' needs are being met.

☐ **Demystify the evaluation process.** New teachers are often quite concerned about how they will be evaluated. In the current political environment in many states around the nation, the process of teacher evaluation has become controversial. Many states tie student achievement data to the evaluation process, and some seek to connect teacher pay to student outcomes. As a result, new teachers will appreciate specific, concrete information about the nuts and bolts of the evaluation process, including when they'll be evaluated, what rubric or system will be used for the evaluation, and how they'll receive feedback about their performance.

Skilled Mentors

KEY IDEA: New teachers who have skilled and supportive mentors are more likely to stay in the profession (Smith & Ingersoll, 2004). However, merely assigning mentors to new teachers does not guarantee that they will get the support they need for a successful transition into the profession. Novice teachers need mentors who understand their unique needs and are equipped with the resources, knowledge, and skills to help them navigate early-career challenges.

The main method schools and districts use to support the success and development of new teachers is assigning mentors (Fulton et al., 2005). Although mentoring program elements vary significantly across states and districts, mentoring is most commonly defined as the establishment of a formal working relationship between a veteran and a novice teacher (Strong, 2005). In practice, mentoring programs range from formal to informal, paid to nonpaid, with training

ranging from extensive to nonexistent. Despite these varia-
tions, however, all mentors share the common goal of helping new teachers experience success during their transition
into the profession.

When beginning teachers have supportive and skilled
mentors, they are more likely to stay in the profession and
express satisfaction with their choice of a career. Having
a mentor also reduces the negative effects of early-career
stress and increases novice teachers' sense of efficacy and
effectiveness (Beam, 2009; Onchwari, 2006). The mentor-
protégé relationship has a positive influence on the mentor as well: according to Hammer (2005), mentors of new
teachers experience increased job satisfaction and renewed
professional growth.

School leaders, district administrators, and anyone else
in charge of overseeing a mentoring program should carefully consider the elements of effective mentor-protégé relationships. The following "to-do" list, while not intended to
be comprehensive, provides an excellent starting point for
creating or evaluating a mentoring program.

☐ **Carefully select mentors with the right characteristics.** The personality traits of the mentor are extremely important; in fact, selecting who will serve as mentors is perhaps one of the principal or program leader's most important responsibilities when it comes to crafting new-teacher supports. Too often, mentors are chosen based on two factors: (1) how long they have been teaching and (2) their teaching assignment. In other words, an experienced 9th grade teacher would be the default selection to mentor a new 9th grade teacher, regardless of the veteran teacher's personality traits or abilities. Picking mentors according to these sole criteria is at best shortsighted and at worst a drastic mistake. Instead, recruit those who possess the characteristics that will enable them to work effectively with new teachers, including

- A positive demeanor.
- An optimistic view of the teaching profession.
- Strong listening skills.
- The ability to model professionalism.
- Flexibility and openness to new ideas.
- Reliability and follow-through on commitments and promises.
- A nonjudgmental attitude in interactions with colleagues.

Note that this list focuses on personality traits and tangible skills rather than on content knowledge or familiarity with grade-level standards. In a perfect world, mentors would possess both sets of skills, but the latter should be only one small consideration when selecting a mentor.

☐ **Ensure that mentors receive training.** After the right people are selected to serve as mentors, they must receive training and ongoing support. Although being a mentor may seem easy in theory, the reality of providing support to a new teacher can be complex and demanding. Although a full discussion of mentor training programs is beyond the scope of this book, the training's essential purpose is to help mentors understand how to support the development of a novice teacher. Most important, they must realize that they are providing support to an adult, professional colleague— not a child. The study of teaching adults, sometimes referred to *andragogy* (as opposed to pedagogy), reminds us that adult learners have special needs and perspectives that are distinct from those of child learners (Knowles, 1980). It is crucial for mentors to acknowledge that new teachers are capable of making their own decisions and managing what takes place in their classrooms. Mentees should be patiently guided through constructive feedback and honest conversation, not controlled or "motivated" to act a certain way. Mentors need to recognize that their role is to guide and support the new teacher, not to create a "mini-me" who behaves and teaches in the same exact way as the mentor.

☐ **Meet with mentors before the start of the school year.** Before the beginning of the school year (or before mentors and new teachers formally meet for the first time), principals should meet with mentors to communicate expectations regarding meeting schedules, topics to be covered, and expected methods of interactions. Remember that assigning a mentor to a new teacher is only the beginning. The job of the principal and the school's leadership team will be to coach and guide mentors as they work to support the new teachers.

☐ **Create the expectation of confidentiality.** Remind mentors that relationships with mentees are most effective when they are confidential. New teachers need to have the assurance that if they speak with their mentors about areas of concern, anxieties, or fears, the information will remain private. This means that the mentor will not be reporting the new teacher's struggles to the administration. Of course, positive feedback and successes are appropriate to share, but it's best to highlight such achievements when the new teacher is present. Novice teachers need to be able to trust that their mentors are not talking behind their backs; there are few things worse for new teachers than to think that people are gossiping about their struggles. Remember that it is natural for most beginning teachers to struggle with classroom management, student behavior, organization, and communication.

☐ **Discuss when to break confidentiality.** Although the mentor-protégé relationship is expected to remain confidential, there may be times when the mentor needs to seek the guidance or support of the administration. Generally, mentors should notify the administration if they have concerns about the ethical or legal behaviors of the new teacher or if there is a concern about student safety. Any other issues that are important enough for the mentor to bring to the principal should already have been addressed with the new teacher. For example, if there are serious organizational concerns that are impeding the new teacher's ability to teach (or his or her colleagues' ability to teach), the mentor should make multiple attempts to resolve the issue directly with the new teacher before talking to the principal. In cases where the mentor believes it necessary to consult the principal, the protégé should be fully aware of and involved in the process. Because the ultimate goal is to provide support and assistance to the new teacher, he or she should be included in all discussions.

☐ **Have ongoing meetings with mentors.** It should be the practice of the principal or district-level leadership to meet regularly with mentors to continue cultivating their professional growth and fostering collaboration. The emphasis of these meetings should be on helping mentors sharpen their communication and relationship skills. Because the mentor-protégé relationship is designed to be confidential, these meetings should not focus on the specific problems one mentor may be having with his or her protégé. The meetings' purpose is to improve mentors' skills, not to provide a forum for griping about new teachers' lack of skills.

So what, specifically, should mentors *do* when they meet with their mentees? While there are many organizations and publications that provide detailed guidance on content or topics mentors can share and discuss with new teachers, the following list provides a basic outline of the most effective things mentors can do to support their protégés.

- **Accept.** The most effective mentors accept the fact that new teachers often have numerous questions and require a good amount of attention, which means that mentors will invest considerable time and energy in the process of helping new teachers during their transition into the profession. Effective mentors embrace the opportunity to positively influence their protégés.

- **Model.** New teachers will be more influenced by the actions and behaviors of their mentors and colleagues than they will by the stated rules or expectations that come from administration. Good mentors serve as examples of professionalism and collegiality and recognize their responsibility to model the behaviors that will help ensure the success of their protégés.

- **Encourage.** There are times when the teaching profession feels lonely, frustrating, and burdensome. The demands and expectations placed on our newest teachers can be overwhelming and lead some to question their choice of career. Mentors should regularly take the time to encourage and build confidence in their protégés—for example, by delivering pep talks, giving thank-you notes or small gifts, or accompanying the new teacher during particularly difficult times.

- **Orient.** Being new to an organization means that the novice must learn how "things are done." Mentors can orient new teachers to tasks and expectations that may be overlooked by veteran staff members as being glaringly obvious, such as staff parking, lunch protocols, staff-meeting norms, how to complete requests for supplies, and what to do when the photocopier jams.

- **Enhance.** Mentors walk a fine line between being directive and being supportive. Although effective mentors recognize that they are supporting an adult learner who can exercise control and choice, they also understand that new teachers often need assistance with lesson planning, managing student behavior, and organization. As a result, mentors should always seek to help their protégés refine and improve their practice. They can achieve this by helping novice teachers plan lessons and solve immediate problems as well as by listening to determine whether action is required or the new teacher merely needs a sympathetic ear.

- **Advocate.** By definition, an advocate is someone who looks out for the best interest of someone else. An advocate serves as a champion and, at times, may speak up to ensure equity. The mentor-as-advocate makes sure that the needs of the new teacher are being met. Beginning teachers often feel reluctant to rock the boat or cause conflict, so they may be inclined to accept suboptimal situations. Advocating for new teachers may also involve protecting protégés from particularly negative or pessimistic individuals on campus.

- **Prepare.** During their first few months in the profession, new teachers experience many "firsts," including open houses, parent-teacher conferences, phone calls home, report cards, and formal evaluations. Although veteran teachers may be proficient and knowledgeable in handling these situations, new teachers often need assistance in preparing for these events. Mentors can walk their protégés through new processes and help them know what to expect.

Helpful Colleagues

KEY IDEA: New teachers who experience strong support from colleagues stay in the profession longer (Benson-Jaja, 2010; Kardos & Johnson, 2007). The support, guidance, resources, and feedback provided by colleagues are more important than most administrators or veteran teachers realize. In fact, some research (Harris, 2013) suggests that colleagues are more influential than are mentors in a new teacher's decision to stay in or leave the profession.

In addition to the rich base of literature surrounding the roles of the principal and the mentor in supporting new teachers, researchers (Johnson & Birkeland, 2003; Kardos & Johnson, 2007) have also considered the influence colleagues have on the retention of novice teachers. Although the assignment of a mentor is the most prominent method of supporting new teachers, mentoring alone—regardless of how good it is—may not be sufficient to address the problem of new-teacher attrition (Ingersoll & Strong, 2011). Among the more interesting findings is the fact that the behavior of veteran teachers plays a significant role in new teachers' view of the profession and their ultimate decision of whether to stay or leave.

Why are colleagues so influential? There could be many reasons, but let's consider the psychological concept known as *social proof*. Social proof refers to our tendency to look to the behavior of others to help us determine our own behavior. Seeing others taking a certain course of action has a tremendous influence on our own decision-making process.

Examples of social proof surround us every day: most of us want to see the latest movie everyone is talking about and drive with the flow of traffic regardless of the posted speed limit. In a school setting, new teachers are constantly observing the behavior of their veteran colleagues when deciding on their own actions. If veteran teachers grumble about students and parents, gossip about one another, arrive late to staff meetings, or generally speak ill of the profession, new teachers will be less likely to want to continue teaching in such an environment. Although the behavior of others is not absolute in its power—there certainly are times when we go against the current—school leadership and veteran colleagues must understand that they have a tremendous influence on new teachers.

Supporting new teachers is everyone's job. Principals cannot do it alone; mentors cannot do it alone. The creation of a collaborative, collegial environment that supports new teachers is the responsibility of all members of the school community (Kardos & Johnson, 2007). Fortunately, there are many practical ways in which experienced teachers can support the growth and retention of their new colleagues. The following list includes some of these.

☐ **Collaborate.** Smith and Ingersoll (2004) found that new teachers who were given regularly scheduled time to collaborate and interact with their colleagues had a much greater likelihood of staying in the profession. In a study of novice teachers' perceptions of school-based supports, Warsame (2011) found that collaboration with colleagues was more helpful than administrative support or professional development. Novice teachers want not only to learn from their more experienced colleagues but also to be viewed as professionals who have important ideas to share. They don't just want to receive feedback and ideas; they want to contribute them as valued members of the team.

☐ **Reduce isolation.** In the traditional education model, teachers act as solo practitioners who are granted broad discretion and control over what happens in the classroom. Unfortunately, this isolation can lead to many of the challenges and failures that teachers experience early in their careers and may be one of the primary reasons new teachers leave the profession (Heller, 2004; Johnson & Birkeland, 2003). Teaching is too complex and challenging to be mastered in seclusion. Experienced teachers can help mitigate the negative effects of isolation by opening their own classrooms for observation, inviting novice colleagues to participate in social events outside school, and helping new teachers plan for instruction. Although veteran teachers often prefer to work alone and exercise high levels of autonomy, recent research has found that new teachers crave a collaborative atmosphere in which they can share ideas, debrief lessons, and reflect on successes (Johnson, 2006).

☐ **Provide emotional support.** New teachers experience many contrasting emotions and often struggle to balance the demands of the profession (Moir, 2009). Experienced colleagues can help to ameliorate these challenges by serving as a sounding board for their less experienced colleagues and helping them to understand that their feelings are normal.

☐ **Observe one another.** We know that new teachers value collaboration and aspire to be viewed as full-fledged members of the school community. One way to simultaneously provide feedback on novice teachers' practice and solicit their ideas and suggestions is to participate in reciprocal classroom observations. These peer observations do not need to be formal or lengthy; their purpose is to enable veteran teachers to see their less experienced colleagues in action and new teachers in turn to observe experienced teachers' practice. Both veteran and novice teachers can learn a few new things from this process, and new teachers get the added benefit of feeling less isolated.

☐ **Plan a lesson together.** Sharing lesson ideas, strategies, handouts, and resources is a valuable and tangible way for veteran teachers to support their less experienced colleagues. Even more powerful, however, is the process of planning and implementing a lesson *with* the new teacher. Work with the new teacher through the process of planning a lesson— from the initial determination of a learning objective to the selection of an assessment technique. Model the processes of deciding which materials to use and differentiating instruction for diverse learners. In other words, give the new teacher a glimpse into the thinking and planning that go into creating a lesson. After the new teacher delivers the lesson, spend some time debriefing successes and challenges he or she experienced. This collaborative planning process is one of the most powerful and effective professional development experiences a new teacher can have.

Additional Tangible Supports

In addition to a quality induction program and the support of administrators, mentors, and colleagues, there are many other tangible and cost-effective ways schools can support early-career teachers. The following list includes tasks that can be carried out by the administrative team, mentors, colleagues, or central office staff, or (most likely) a combination of these personnel.

☐ Ensure that the new teacher's classroom is clean and decluttered (with the previous teacher's materials removed or organized) at least a week prior to his or her scheduled start date. Make sure to check the file cabinets and storage areas. It should not be the responsibility of the new teacher to clean, organize, or figure out what to do with the previous teacher's "stuff."

☐ Complete a supply order for the new teacher and have materials ready in the classroom, including paper, pencils, markers, staplers, and file folders. New teachers should not have to feel embarrassed to ask for the supplies they need to set up their classrooms. In addition, ensure that curricular materials are placed in a visible location in the new teacher's classroom on the first day. It can be very frustrating for a new teacher to have to hunt for the appropriate curricular materials.

☐ Orient the new teacher to the school, giving a tour and explaining whom he or she should contact with the inevitable questions about supplies, technology, and school procedures. Answer such questions as *Where do I park? Where can I leave my lunch? Where do I get supplies? When is the building open? What is the alarm code if I come in on the weekend? Do I make my own copies, or does someone do that for us? Whom do I contact if I am sick and can't come to work? Whom should I talk to if I have computer problems?*

☐ If the teacher is new to town, inform him or her about places to live, shopping areas, doctor's offices, gyms, restaurants, childcare options, parks, and other important locations and resources.

☐ Remember that money may be tight for some new teachers, and in most cases, they will not receive a paycheck until after they have been working for several weeks. Think before asking them to contribute to social funds, purchase school shirts, or participate in any other initiative that requires money. Even "optional" activities come with social pressure.

☐ Review class lists prior to distribution to the new teachers. Make sure the lists are equitable in terms of gender and fair when it comes to 504 students or special education students, students with disciplinary issues, and student achievement. Remember that *fair* doesn't necessarily mean *the same*; consider sheltering new teachers from the full workload required of veteran teachers. Allow them to ease in to the more difficult parts of the profession, and avoid giving them more "challenging" or high-needs students than veteran teachers have.

☐ Be mindful of the different "firsts" the new teacher will experience throughout the year—for example, parent-teacher conferences, progress reports, teacher evaluations, holiday parties, family nights, and field trips—and arrange for appropriate support during each.

☐ Outline all the responsibilities new teachers will have on the very first day of school. Review expectations for greeting students in the morning, completing lunch counts, reporting attendance, and dismissing students at the end of the day. Also work with them to create a to-do list of important things to accomplish during their first few weeks of school. For example, provide important dates for them to place on their calendars and help them schedule when to send out their first parent newsletter.

☐ Provide small gifts and thank-you notes periodically throughout the year to encourage the new teacher. This can be especially powerful during times when the teacher will likely be overwhelmed with the job's expectations and requirements (e.g., parent-teacher conferences, formal evaluations, and report cards).

To give your feedback on this publication and be entered into a drawing for a free ASCD Arias e-book, please visit
www.ascd.org/ariasfeedback

ENCORE

PHASES OF A FIRST-YEAR TEACHER

Any discussion about supporting new teachers would be incomplete without acknowledging the work of Ellen Moir and the New Teacher Center. Moir's (1990) seminal work, "Phases of First-Year Teaching," offered one of the first research-based examinations of the lives of new teachers. This article has served as a foundation for much of the more recent research focused on helping new teachers transition into the profession.

Moir found that most new teachers go through several distinct phases during their first year of teaching (see Figure 1). In her work with the New Teacher Project at the University of California, Santa Cruz, Moir studied these phases and their possible impact on teacher attrition and retention and advised support providers, mentors, and administrators to gain an understanding of these common phases, which are as follows.

1. **Anticipation.** This phase is characterized by the excitement new teachers experience upon being hired for a teaching position. According to Moir's findings, this phase begins during the student teaching period; preservice teachers tend to romanticize the role of teacher. Moir (1999) observes, "New teachers enter classrooms with a tremendous commitment to making a difference and a somewhat idealistic view of how to accomplish their goals."

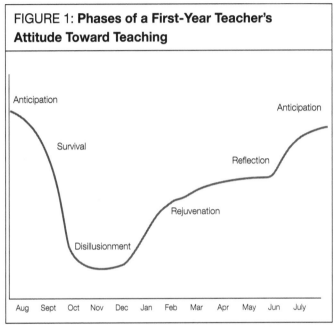

FIGURE 1: **Phases of a First-Year Teacher's Attitude Toward Teaching**

Anticipation

Anticipation

Survival

Reflection

Rejuvenation

Disillusionment

Aug   Sept   Oct   Nov   Dec   Jan   Feb   Mar   Apr   May   Jun   July

Source: From "The stages of a teacher's first year," by E. Moir, in M. Scherer (Ed.), *A better beginning: Supporting and mentoring new teachers* (pp. 19–23), 1999, Alexandria, VA: ASCD.

2. **Survival.** Moir (1990) points out that "despite teacher preparation programs, new teachers are caught off guard by the realities of teaching." During this phase, new teachers turn their attention to managing the day-to-day routines and challenges of teaching. They often report putting in long hours as they attempt to navigate this new world that involves managing classrooms, developing curriculum, building collegial relationships, and dispatching administrative duties.

3. **Disillusionment.** After six to eight weeks of the survival phase, new teachers typically enter the disillusionment phase. They tend to experience self-doubt during this period and wonder whether they made the right decision to enter the teaching profession. Adding to their stress is the fact that parent-teacher conferences often take place during this time.

4. **Rejuvenation.** The rejuvenation phase is characterized by a gradual positive shift in the new teacher's attitude toward the profession. It often arises after the winter break, when rest, family connections, and time away from the classroom offer new teachers the chance to place their career and classroom practice into perspective.

5. **Reflection.** With most of a year's experience under their belt, new teachers often enter a period of self-reflection, when they are able to review the highlights, successes, and challenges of the school year. Because the end of the year is in sight, they begin envisioning what their second year will be like.

Although not all teachers experience the phases described here—or in the same order or at the same level of intensity—these phases are indicative of the overall teacher experience and are prevalent within the broader teaching community (Moir, 1999). An understanding of these phases, taken together with this book's strategies for induction and support, can help ensure that all new teachers will receive the support they need to stay in the profession.

Extend Your Knowledge

To learn more about mentoring and induction programs, check out the following resources.

- *The 21st Century Mentor's Handbook: Creating a Culture for Learning* by Paula Rutherford. (2005). Alexandria, VA: Just ASK Publications.
- *A Better Beginning: Supporting and Mentoring New Teachers* by Marge Scherer (Ed.). (1999). Alexandria, VA: ASCD.
- *Becoming a High-Performance Mentor: A Guide to Reflection and Action* by James B. Rowley. (2006). Thousand Oaks, CA: Corwin.
- *Being an Effective Mentor: How to Help Beginning Teachers Succeed* by Kathleen Feeney Jonson. (2002). Thousand Oaks, CA: Corwin.
- *Effective Teacher Induction and Mentoring: Assessing the Evidence* by Michael Strong. (2009). New York: Teachers College Press.
- *Leading the Teacher Induction and Mentoring Program* by Barry W. Sweeny. (2008). Thousand Oaks, CA: Corwin.
- *Maximum Mentoring: An Action Guide for Teacher Trainers and Cooperating Teachers* by Gwen L. Rudney and Andrea M. Guillaume. (2003). Thousand Oaks, CA: Corwin.
- *Mentoring New Teachers* by Hal Portner. (2008). Thousand Oaks, CA: Corwin.

- *New Teacher Induction: How to Train, Support, and Retain New Teachers* by Annette L. Breaux and Harry K. Wong. (2003). Mountain View, CA: Harry K. Wong Publications.
- *New Teacher Mentoring: Hopes and Promise for Improving Teacher Effectiveness* by Ellen Moir, Dara Barlin, Janet Gless, and Jan Miles. (2009). Cambridge, MA: Harvard Education Press.
- *The Reflective Educator's Guide to Mentoring: Strengthening Practice Through Knowledge, Story, and Metaphor* by Diane Yendol-Hoppey and Nancy Fichtman Dana. (2007). Thousand Oaks, CA: Corwin.
- *Successful Induction for New Teachers: A Guide for NQTs and Induction Tutors, Coordinators and Mentors* by Sara Bubb. (2007). Thousand Oaks, CA: SAGE Publications.

References

Barth, R. (2013). The time is ripe (again). *Educational Leadership, 71*(2), 10–16.

Bartlett, L., & Johnson, L. (2010). The evolution of new teacher induction policy. *Educational Policy, 24*(6), 847–871.

Beam, P. (2009). *Investigation of needs/concerns of teachers within an induction year program* (Doctoral dissertation). Retrieved from Ohio-LINK. (ohiou1236949276).

Benson-Jaja, L. (2010). *Evaluation of the impact of effective mentoring on teacher retention* (Doctoral dissertation). Retrieved from PQDT Open. (UMI 3463468).

Breaux, A. L., & Wong, H. K. (2003). *New teacher induction: How to train, support, and retain new teachers.* Mountain View, CA: Harry K. Wong Publications.

Darling-Hammond, L. (2005). Prepping our teachers for teaching as a profession. *Phi Delta Kappan, 87,* 237–240.

Darling-Hammond, L. (2013). When teachers support and evaluate their peers. *Educational Leadership, 71*(2), 24–29.

Darling-Hammond, L., & Sykes, G. (2003). Wanted: A national teacher supply policy for education. *Education Policy Analysis Archives, 11*(33), 1–55.

Fulton, K., Yoon, I., & Lee, C. (2005). Induction into learning communities. *Education, 126*(4), 653–659.

Graue, E., & Rauscher, E. (2009). Researcher perspectives on class size reduction. *Education Policy Analysis Archives, 17*(9).

Hammer, M. D. (2005). Rejuvenating retirees: Mentoring first-year teachers. *Delta Kappa Gamma Bulletin, 71*(4), 20–25.

Harris, B. (2013). *Retention of novice teachers who relocate to Arizona to begin their teaching careers* (Unpublished doctoral dissertation, Bethel University, St. Paul, Minnesota).

Heller, D. A. (2004). *Teachers wanted: Attracting and retaining good teachers.* Alexandria, VA: ASCD.

Huisman, S., Singer, N., & Catapano, S. (2010). Resiliency to success: Supporting novice urban teachers. *Teacher Development, 14*(4), 483–499.

Ingersoll, R. (2001, Fall). Teacher turnover and teacher shortages: An organizational analysis. *American Educational Research Journal, 38*(3), 499–534.

Ingersoll, R., & Strong, M. (2011). The impact of induction and mentoring programs for beginning teachers: A critical review of the research. *Review of Educational Research, 81*(2), 201–233.

Johnson, S. M. (2006, July). *The workplace matters: Teacher quality, retention, and effectiveness.* Washington, DC: National Education Association. Retrieved from http://files.eric.ed.gov/fulltext/ED495822.pdf

Johnson, S. M., & Birkeland, S. E. (2003). The schools that teachers choose. *Educational Leadership, 60*(8), 20–24.

Kardos, S., & Johnson, S. (2007). On their own and presumed expert: New teachers' experience with their colleagues. *Teachers College Record, 109*(9), 2083–2106.

Kardos, S., Johnson, S., Peske, H., Kauffman, D., & Liu, E. (2001). Counting on colleagues: New teachers encounter the professional culture of their schools. *Education Administration Quarterly, 27*(2), 250–290.

Knowles, M. (1980). *The modern practice of adult education: From andragogy to pedagogy.* New York: Follett.

Markow, D., & Martin, S. (2005). *The MetLife survey of the American teacher: Transitions and the role of supportive relationships.* Retrieved from http://files.eric.ed.gov/fulltext/ED488837.pdf

Moir, E. (1990). The phases of first-year teaching. Newsletter for the California New Teacher Project. Sacramento, CA: California Department of Education.

Moir, E. (1999). The stages of a teacher's first year. In M. Scherer (Ed.), *A better beginning: Supporting and mentoring new teachers* (pp. 19–23). Alexandria, VA: ASCD.

Moir, E. (2009). Accelerating teacher effectiveness: Lessons learned from two decades of new teacher induction. *Phi Delta Kappan, 91*(2), 14–21.

Onchwari, G. (2006, Summer). Benefits of mentoring: Head Start teacher perceptions of the effectiveness of a local implementation of a teacher professional development initiative. *Essays in Education Online Journal, 17.* Retrieved from http://www.usca.edu/essays/vol172006/onchwaritext.pdf

Reiman, A., & Corbell, K. (2007). *Beginning teachers' perceptions of success: A summary report for Northeast Collaborative Effort to Support Initially Licensed Professionals.* College of Education, North Carolina State University. Retrieved from http://www.necollaborative.org/docs/PSI-BT%20Northeast%20Collaborative%20%20Final%20report.pdf

Smith, T., & Ingersoll, R. (2004). Reducing teacher turnover: What are the components of effective induction? *American Educational Research Journal, 41,* 687–714.

Strong, M. (2005). Induction, mentoring, and retention: A summary of the research. *New Educator, 1*(3), 181–198.

Tirozzi, G. N., Carbonaro, P., & Winters, M. (2014, April 25). *Addressing a shortage of high quality teachers: An escalating dilemma for Arizona Schools.* Phoenix, AZ: Grand Canyon University College of Doctoral Studies. Retrieved from http://www.gcu.edu/Documents/addressing%20a%20shortage%20of%20high%20quality%20teachers.pdf

Warsame, K. B. (2011). *Evaluating the effectiveness of novice teacher support structures.* (Doctoral dissertation). Retrieved from PQDT Open. (3443670).

Zumwalt, K., & Craig, E. (2005). Teachers' characteristics: Research on the demographic profile. In M. Cochran-Smith & K. M. Zeichner (Eds.), *Studying teacher education: The report of the AERA Panel on Research and Teacher Education* (pp. 111–149). Mahwah, NJ: Lawrence Erlbaum Associates.

Related ASCD Resources

At the time of publication, the following ASCD resources were available (ASCD stock numbers appear in parentheses). For up-to-date information about ASCD resources, go to www.ascd.org. You can search the complete archives of Educational Leadership at http://www.ascd.org/el.

ASCD EDge®
Exchange ideas and connect with other educators interested in teacher retention on the social networking site ASCD EDge at edge.ascd.org.

Print Products
100+ Ways to Recognize and Reward Your School Staff by Emily E. Houck (#112051)

A Better Beginning: Supporting and Mentoring New Teachers by Marge Scherer (Ed.) (#199236E4)

Keeping Good Teachers by Marge Scherer (Ed.) (#104138)

Teachers Wanted: Attracting and Retaining Good Teachers by Daniel A. Heller (#104005)

DVDs
ASCD Master Class Leadership Series (#613026)

The How To Collection: Helping New Teachers (#606142)

The How To Collection: School Leadership (#606140)

ASCD PD Online® Courses
Leadership: Effective Critical Skills (#PD09OC08M)

Leading Professional Learning: Building Capacity Through Teacher Leaders (#PD13OC010M)

For more information: send e-mail to member@ascd.org; call 1-800-933-2723 or 703-578-9600, press 2; send a fax to 703-575-5400; or write to Information Services, ASCD, 1703 N. Beauregard St., Alexandria, VA 22311-1714 USA.

About the Author

Bryan Harris serves as the Director of Professional Development & Public Relations for the Casa Grande (Arizona) Elementary School District. He holds a Bachelor of Science degree in Education and a Master of Educational Leadership degree from Northern Arizona University. In 2013, he earned a doctorate (EdD) from Bethel University in Minnesota after studying factors impacting new-teacher retention. He also holds a certification in brain-based learning from Jensen Learning. Having served in many roles as an educator—from a classroom teacher to a principal and now a central office leader—Bryan understands the challenges teachers and school leaders face as they strive to meet the needs of all students. Each year, he speaks to thousands of educators across the United States on the topics of student engagement, motivation, classroom management, and brain-based learning. He is the author or coauthor of several books, including the popular 2010 book *Battling Boredom*. He can be reached at www.bryan-harris.com.